OCT   2016

D0908879

Refugees

Critical World Issues

CRITICAL WORLD ISSUES

Refugees

Harry Miller

MASON CREST
PHILADELPHIA

Mason Crest
450 Parkway Drive, Suite D
Broomall, PA 19008
www.masoncrest.com

©2017 by Mason Crest, an imprint of National Highlights, Inc.

Printed and bound in the United States of America.

CPSIA Compliance Information: Batch #CWI2016.
For further information, contact Mason Crest at 1-866-MCP-Book.

First printing
1 3 5 7 9 8 6 4 2

Library of Congress Cataloging-in-Publication Data

on file at the Library of Congress
ISBN: 978-1-4222-3660-4 (hc)
ISBN: 978-1-4222-8140-6 (ebook)

Critical World Issues series ISBN: 978-1-4222-3645-1

Table of Contents

KEY ICONS TO LOOK FOR:

 Words to Understand: These words with their easy-to-understand definitions will increase the reader's understanding of the text, while building vocabulary skills.

 Sidebars: This boxed material within the main text allows readers to build knowledge, gain insights, explore possibilities, and broaden their perspectives by weaving together additional information to provide realistic and holistic perspectives.

 Research Projects: Readers are pointed toward areas of further inquiry connected to each chapter. Suggestions are provided for projects that encourage deeper research and analysis.

 Text-Dependent Questions: These questions send the reader back to the text for more careful attention to the evidence presented there.

 Series Glossary of Key Terms: This back-of-the book glossary contains terminology used throughout this series. Words found here increase the reader's ability to read and comprehend higher-level books and articles in this field.

What Is a Refugee?

Mina is a European *refugee* now living in the United States. As a teenager, she was forced to flee her home in Bosnia, part of the former Yugoslavia, during fighting among different ethnic groups. She says:

"My name is Mina Kovacevic, and I am a Muslim from Sarajevo, in Bosnia. In May 1992, two months after the war began, I left my home and homeland. Many of my neighbors had been killed. My mother, father, two sisters, nephew, and I spent twenty-four hours a day in a bomb shelter. We were among forty people — mostly women and children — hiding in a small, dark room listening to the shooting and shelling.

"My sister had been undergoing chemotherapy. But

During the 1990s the country of Yugoslavia, which had been created after World War I, broke apart into many separate countries, accompanied by warfare that targeted civilians. These are a few of the more than 200,000 ethnic Albanians who were displaced during the conflict.

we knew that even if we got her to the hospital, there would be no treatment for her. So we decided to try to leave. Our car and others were stopped by Serb soldiers. They ordered us to pull off to the side of the road and told us we were being held as hostages. The soldiers

 # Words to Understand in This Chapter

asylum—a place of safety and refuge provided by a host country to refugees.

asylum seekers—people who have applied for refugee status and are waiting to see if they will be granted protection as a refugee.

citizen—a member of a country or other political community.

civil war—a war between opposing groups within one country.

convention—a legal agreement to behave in a certain way, made between two or more countries.

deportation—the forced removal of a person from one country to another.

detention center—a place where asylum seekers are held while their cases are investigated.

internally displaced person—a person who has been forced from their home, but is still within their home country's borders.

malnourished—lacking foods necessary for good health.

migrant—someone who moves from one region or country to another.

refugee—person taking refuge, especially in a foreign country to escape such troubles as religious or political persecution and war.

UN (United Nations)—an international organization, founded in 1945, in which representatives from most of the world's nations meet to discuss conflicts and try to work towards peace.

UNHCR—the office of the United Nations High Commissioner for Refugees, set up by the UN to deal with the problem of refugees.

visa—a document or stamp in a passport allowing a person to visit or stay in a country.

Bosnian Muslim refugees pass through a United Nations checkpoint, May 1994.

began making lists of the children in our convoy, threatening to kill them first.

"We spent three nights in our car without food. We saw and heard men being tortured by the soldiers. At night, the soldiers would shine flashlights into our cars while bragging of all the children they had already killed. We were all in terror for my four-year-old nephew.

"Finally, we were allowed to go. When we reached Croatia, the Croats put us in a refugee camp where we

Refugees from Kosovo carry bread to their families in a UN-run camp, 1999.

lived with forty people to a tent. The Croats were not prepared to receive so many people, and after ten days they told us we had to move on to another camp in eastern Slovenia.

"We were the first refugees to arrive in this camp. There were a few huts, and we were lucky enough to be put in one. Even though we shared it with twelve or fourteen strangers, we felt much safer because there was no shooting in the area.

"As summer turned into fall, more refugees arrived. The huts were full, so new arrivals were housed in tents that faced rain, snow, and extreme cold without any heat. Sanitation was deplorable: twenty to thirty toilets and only twenty showers for three thousand people."

After enduring these hardships, Mina's life took a turn for the better. Her family was granted refuge in Denmark, and Mina was given a scholarship to study in the United States. She described this as "the greatest thing I could imagine." Since then, she has completed a degree in psychology and hopes to return to her homeland if the situation there remains stable.

Albanian refugees follow a railroad line while fleeing their homeland, 1999.

Mina is just one of millions of refugees found all over the world. Many face an uncertain future.

What Is a Refugee?

First and foremost, a refugee is a person who is in need of help. The Merriam-Webster dictionary defines a *refugee* as "someone who has been forced to leave a country because of war or for religious or political reasons."

The most important definition of a refugee, however, is the one set forth in the 1951 *United Nations Convention* Relating to the Status of Refugees. Twenty-six governments, including the United States, Canada, France, Germany, the United Kingdom, and Australia drafted this convention, or treaty, to ensure that all human beings, including refugees, "shall enjoy fundamental rights and freedoms without discrimination." It defines a refugee as:

> A person who owing to a well-founded fear of being persecuted for reasons of race, religion, nationality, membership of a particular social group or political opinion, is outside the country of his nationality and is unable or, owing to such fear, is unwilling to avail himself of the protection of that country; or who, not having a nationality and being outside the country of his former habitual residence as a result of such events, is unable or, owing to such fear, is unwilling to return to it.

At the time this convention was signed, members were concerned about the people who'd fled their homes during World

In 1946, delegates of fourteen nations met to discuss efforts to repatriate and resettle European refugees after the Second World War, and to provide for their care and maintenance while awaiting re-establishment. This Preparatory Commission International Refugee Organization would become a body of the newly formed United Nations.

Palestinian Arabs who are fleeing conflict in their homeland wait for transportation that will take them over the border into Lebanon, 1948. When Great Britain pulled out of Palestine, and Israel declared its independence, several hundred thousand Arabs left their homes to escape from the conflict.

War II, so they limited the definition to those who had fled "events occurring before 1 January 1951" and "events occurring in Europe." Members removed those restrictions in a later version called the 1967 Protocol Relating to the Status of Refugees, but allowed those countries that signed the 1951 version to retain the restriction. In 2001 the United Nations issued another declaration signed by the original signatories to the convention, reaffirming their commitment to the 1951 Convention and the 1967 Protocol.

As of 2016, 145 states have signed the 1951 convention, 146 have signed the 1967 protocol, and 142 states have signed both the convention and the protocol. To this day, the convention's definition of a refugee is the one that many countries and international organizations use to determine who qualifies as a refugee.

Syrian Refugees and migrants stage a protest demanding to be allowed to cross to Macedonia, near the Greek village of Idomeni.

Northern Alliance fighters drive through the front line during the war in Afghanistan against the Taliban. As soldiers, they cannot be called refugees.

Confusing Terms

The terms *migrant, asylum seeker,* and *refugee* are sometimes used interchangeably, but there are important legal distinctions between these terms.

A refugee is a person who has fled his or her country to escape war or persecution. The 1951 Convention Relating to the Status of Refugees says that such a person is entitled to protection, so long as they can prove that they truly meet the "refugee" definition. Because that person is a refugee, another country's government can grant him or her permission to live in their country.

Anyone who moves from one country to another is considered a migrant unless he or she is specifically fleeing war or persecution. Migrants may be trying to escape from extreme poverty, or they may be seeking better opportunities or hoping to join relatives who have gone before them. The difference between a refugee and a migrant is that the migrant who does not have appropriate documentation can be deported by the country where he or she has migrated. The International Organization for Migration, or IOM, has estimated that more than 232 million people migrate from one country to another each year.

Like migrants, asylum seekers move from one place to another in search of *asylum*, or safety. They may ask for protection as refugees, but may or may not necessarily meet the criteria set forth in the 1951 convention. These people are called asylum seekers while they await determination of their status, according to the United Nations Educational, Scientific, and Cultural Organization (UNESCO).

The application process for an asylum seeker to be accepted into the United States as a refugee can take between 18 and 24 months. "In order to ensure safety and security within American communities where those in need are welcomed, each refugee admitted into the US undergoes the highest cate-

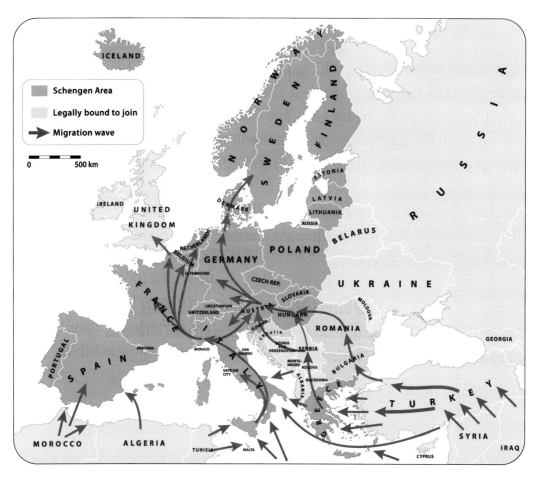

An influx of refugees fleeing from the Syrian civil war, from sectarian fighting in Iraq, and from repressive governments in North Africa has led to a migration crisis in Europe that began in 2015. Refugees are trying to reach the so-called Schengen Area—a group of countries in the European Union that have eliminated most border controls. Germany, Hungary, Sweden, and Austria were the most popular destinations for refugees.

A family of Canadian Muslims hold signs at Toronto's Pearson International Airport, welcoming the first Syrian refugees to the country in 2015.

gory of security screening for entering the country," says a statement on the White House website.

Challenges Asylum Seekers Face

In the U.S., asylum status is granted to those who meet the definition of a refugee, which means they have been persecuted for their race, religion, nationality, political opinion, or membership in a particular social group and are already in the country or waiting at a port of entry, such as an airport, according to Refugee Council USA.

Refugees from Syria, Afghanistan, and Africa arrive at the Greek island of Lesvos, 2016. They came aboard a small boat from Turkey.

Unfortunately, upon arrival, many asylum seekers are detained in short-term holding cells or jail-like *detention centers* for days, weeks, or even months.

"Receiving asylum in the United States can be a lifeline to safety and provide a path to healing, but when asylum seekers arrive at a U.S. border or port of entry, they are frequently shocked at the treatment they endure upon reaching 'safety' and 'protection,' as they are arrested, shackled, and confined," said a report issued by the Center for Victims of Torture, The Torture Abolition and Survivor Support Coalition, and The

Unitarian Universalist Service Committee titled *Tortured and Detained: Survivor Stories of U.S. Immigration Detention.* "[I]n less than three years—from October 2010 to February 2013—the United States detained approximately 6,000 survivors of torture as they were seeking asylum protection."

A February 4, 2015, *New York Times* article drew attention to a southeastern New Mexico detention center, where hundreds of women and children were confined to metal trailers surrounded by barbed wire.

"A detainee in Artesia named Sofia explained that a gang murdered her brother, shot her husband, and then kidnapped and raped her 14-year-old stepdaughter," the article said. "A Guatemalan woman named Kira said that she fled when a gang targeted her family over their involvement in a nonviolence movement at church; when Kira's husband went into hiding, the gang subjected her to repeated sexual assaults and threatened to cut her unborn baby from her womb. An inmate named Marisol said she crossed the U.S. border in June after a gang in Honduras murdered the father of her 3-year-old twins, then turned its attention to her."

When they arrived in the U.S., they were forced to sleep four families to a room in deplorable conditions. Their children came down with chickenpox, tonsillitis, and fevers.

"Many were under the age of 6 and had been raised on a diet of tortillas, rice, and chicken bits. [But in] Artesia, the institutional cafeteria foods were as unfamiliar as the penal atmosphere, and to their parents' horror, many of the children refused to eat," the article said. Children became *malnourished* and sickly. "As the months ticked by in Artesia, many detainees began to wonder if they would ever be free again."

The United States is not the only country that detains asylum seekers. Of the 21,843 people who applied for asylum in the United Kingdom of Great Britain in 2012, more than 11 percent were detained, according to *UNHCR*. In 2013, 203 children—155 of whom were under age 11—were detained. Asylum seekers in Europe have been fingerprinted, numbered with permanent marker, and photographed.

"Groups including the UN refugee agency (UNHCR) and Amnesty International have urged nations to stop 'processing' vulnerable men, women, and children like criminals," the British newspaper *Independent* said in a September 2, 2015, article.

Elsewhere, asylum seekers are forced to live with criminals. In July 2015, an Australian newspaper reported that 448 killers, rapists, and other criminals awaiting *deportation* for their crime or for overstaying their *visa* were being kept alongside asylum seekers in detention centers. Instead of separating the groups, the government introduced a bill that gives security guards the authority to use whatever force they see fit. A spokeswoman for an Australian government official told the *Sydney Morning Herald* that "the government used the presence of criminals in detention to justify 'laws that allow guards to brutalize anyone in the camps.'"

As seen in some European countries during the Syrian *civil war* and resulting refugee crisis, asylum seekers have not been welcomed with open arms in Australia. In January 2014, the *Sydney Morning Herald* reported results from a UMR Research poll that revealed "only 30 percent of Australians believe that most asylum seekers are genuine refugees." Sixty percent wanted the government to "increase the severity of the treatment of asylum seekers," and "59 percent oppose refugees receiving government welfare assistance."

In Britain, most financial aid given to asylum seekers comes in the form of vouchers that are valid for four weeks and can only be used in certain stores. Some aid organizations believe

These Syrian refugees in Hungary were unable to bring much with them. Most refugees typically have meager possessions.

vouchers humiliate asylum seekers and mark them as targets for prejudice. One young woman told Oxfam that receiving vouchers was "like getting a stamp saying you don't belong."

Many asylum seekers arrive in host countries poor and in need but were wealthy in their own country. Taking flight typically means abandoning everything one owns or having it taken away. Wars and persecution cut across class and education boundaries, forcing people from all walks of life—from peasant farmers to lawyers and doctors—to flee. Although asylum seekers require aid on arrival, their skills and knowledge may be of positive benefit in the future.

Aren't Most Asylum Seekers Bogus?

Deciding who qualifies as a refugee can be difficult. Cases have to be investigated closely to see if someone has "a well-founded fear of persecution." Refugee status is granted to fewer than half of the asylum seekers who apply in Europe and North America.

Asylum seekers whose applications are turned down are sometimes labeled as "bogus." This is a highly-charged word that implies that the person is dishonest or is attempting to cheat the system in order to obtain a higher standard of living. While it's true that some claims for asylum are groundless, a large number of the adults who seek asylum, including many whose applications are rejected, have suffered human rights abuses and other forms of persecution. In many host countries, between fifteen and thirty-five percent of those who are not granted refugee status are still allowed to remain on "humanitarian grounds."

How Many Refugees Are There?

"Globally, one in every 122 humans is now either a refugee, *internally displaced*, or seeking asylum," UNHCR reported in June 2015. According to its annual *Global Trends Report*, there were 19.5 million refugees, 38.2 million internally displaced persons, and 1.8 million asylum seekers at the end of 2014.

During the Syrian civil war, which began in 2011 and continued into 2016, more than 4.2 million *citizens* fled to Egypt, Iraq, Jordan, Lebanon, Turkey, and other countries, according to the UNHCR. Nearly 8 million others were classified as internally displaced, meaning that they had fled their homes but were still living within Syria.

 Text-Dependent Questions

1. Why do people flee their homeland?
2. What differentiates a migrant from a refugee?

 Research Project

Do you think asylum seekers should be detained when they arrive in a country, such as the U.S.? Some people believe asylum seekers and their children have been traumatized enough in their own country and should be allowed to start a new life without being jailed. Other people are wary of terrorism and believe it's better to be safe than sorry. Using the Internet or your school library, research the plight and treatment of asylum seekers and write a two-page report summarizing your findings and your belief.

What Causes Refugees?

T he United States Constitution provides citizens with *civil rights* that enhance our quality of life and protect us from harm. People who live in other countries are not as fortunate. In fact, as learned from the definition of refugee, governments sometimes indulge in *persecution* and other means that force a political, religious, or ethnic group to flee a country.

Political Repression

People sometimes flee their homeland due to poverty and oppression. For instance, since the late 1990s, tens of thousands of North Koreans have fled to China and South Korea. The country is so behind the times that a doctor who resettles in South Korea must undergo further training before he or she

Many people become refugees to escape repressive governments and harsh living conditions in places like North Korea, Syria, and Iran.

can practice medicine, according to nonprofit organization Liberty in North Korea, which is based in California and South Korea. Few North Koreans have touched a computer or an ATM machine.

"In information-technology terms, North Korea is locked in a time warp," Melanie Kirkpatrick wrote in *Escape from North Korea: The Untold Story of Asia's Underground Railroad*. "Founder Kim Il Sung understood the power of information, and after the Korean War ended, he made sure that his regime had a monopoly on it. . . . None of the modern technologies that connect us to each other and the world at large are available in North Korea. There is no text messaging, no email, no photo sharing, no social networking."

North Korea's capital, Pyongyang, and high-ranking officials obtained cellular service in 2008. A mere four percent of

 Words to Understand in This Chapter

civil rights—basic rights of everyone, including freedom and equality.

civil war—a war between opposing groups within one country.

civilians—people who are not in the armed forces.

forced labor—forcing people to work, usually in terrible conditions.

genocide—the deliberate attempt to kill all of the members of a racial, ethnic, or religious group.

human rights—the basic rights of all human beings, such as the right to free speech, food, and shelter.

Muslim—a person who follows the Islamic religion.

persecution—the harassment and mistreatment of a particular person or group of people because of their beliefs.

North Korean soldiers participate in a military parade.

the country had subscribed by 2012, but the government monitors calls and blocks service to international numbers. When foreigners visit the country, the government confiscates their phone and returns it when they leave.

Likewise, the government restricts the Internet and forbids tuneable radios. Newspapers say what the government tells them to write.

If someone criticizes the government, he or she may be arrested. "[I]f your relative is persecuted for 'anti-state' or 'anti-socialist' crimes, then you and three generations of your family can be punished for it," notes a report from the group Liberty in North Korea. "The aim is to remove from society the whole family unit to prevent any dissent from emerging in the future."

Despite a famine that killed close to a million people in the 1990s, the fact that two-thirds of its population depend on government rations of barley, maize, or rice twice a month in order to eat, and the fact that North Korea depends on donations to make up for the food it does not produce, the country spends about a third of its national income on the military, Reuters reported in 2011. In 2009, that amounted to $570 million. In 2012, the UN reported that one-third of North Korean children under age five had suffered stunted growth as a result of malnutrition. Babies who should have been able to sit up couldn't even hold a bottle.

Still, citizens who would like to provide a better life for their family must ask permission to leave the country or to travel from one part of North Korea to another. Often the request is denied.

Those who are caught fleeing the country face imprisonment, beatings, torture, and *forced labor* upon their return.

On March 21, 2013, the United Nations Human Rights Council created the Commission of Inquiry on Human Rights in the Democratic People's Republic of Korea in order to investigate *human rights* abuses, such as prison camps, kidnappings, and discrimination. After compiling a 372-page report that included "brainwashing, torture, deliberate starvation, executions, and infanticide," per the *Washington Post*, the UN voted to hold the dictatorship accountable. "The nonbinding

Young students in class at the Provincial Boarding School in Hamhung City in the Democratic People's Republic of Korea (North Korea). The government of North Korea spends much of its money on the military, leaving little to help ordinary citizens, and international organizations like the UN Children's Fund (UNICEF) and the World Food Programme (WFP) must step in to help by creating schools and running programs within the country.

In March 2016, the United Nations Security Council voted unanimously to impose sanctions on North Korea because the country had continued working to develop nuclear weapons and ballistic missiles that it could use to threaten neighboring countries.

resolution, led by the European Union and Japan, passed 111 to 19," the *Washington Post* said. "Fifty-five countries abstained."

Religious Persecution

Not surprisingly, North Korea also prevents its twenty-four million people from practicing the religion they believe in.

Forget spreading the Good News in a dictatorship. "Proselytizing in North Korea is life-threatening work," Melanie Kirkpatrick wrote in *Escape from North Korea: The*

Untold Story of Asia's Underground Railroad. One woman, thirty-three-year-old Ri Hyon-ok, was publicly executed in 2009 for distributing bibles. Her husband and three children were sent to a gulag, or forced labor camp. Worshipping Jesus is just as dangerous. Three people were executed after a 2010 raid on the church they held in a private home. Twenty attendees were sentenced to a prison camp.

Christianity is not the only faith being persecuted, and North Korea is not the only country doing the persecuting, however. During an October 2015 speech to UNHCR's executive committee, UN High Commissioner for Refugees António

African Christians participate in a church service under a tree in South Sudan. Christians have been persecuted in this region for many years.

Guterres said *Muslims* account for two-thirds of the world's refugees. That number includes the Rohingya people, who live in the state of Rakhine, Myanmar, in Southeast Asia.

Despite the fact generations of Rohingya people have lived in Burma, the government stripped them of their citizenship in 1982. Since then, they have been denied all the rights that citizenship entails. For instance, they cannot vote. They were prevented them from taking part in the first census in thirty years. They're even forbidden from becoming doctors or lawyers.

Buddhists have persecuted Rohingya Muslims for decades. Then, in 2012, "religious and ethnic tensions between the

Rohingya refugees living in Malaysia wait for food to be distributed by a local non-governmental organization.

Rohingya refugees demonstrate against persecution in Myanmar as part of the World Refugee Rally in Brisbane, Australia, June 2015.

Royingya Muslims and the Rakhine Buddhists, who make up the majority of the population, escalated into widespread, deadly rioting," according to Amnesty International Australia. "In an attempt to flee the violence, the Rohingya people have become among the world's least wanted [and] denied resettlement in Indonesia, Thailand, Bangladesh, Malaysia, or Australia."

Nearly ninety thousand Rohingyas fled. One hundred and forty thousand have been isolated inside guarded camps for

Many Rohingya Muslims who have become refugees from persecution in Myanmar live in substandard housing in refugee camps such as this one in Sittwe.

internally displaced people, where they have been subjected to forced labor, torture, rape, and executions.

Ethnic Cleansing and Genocide

Some governments have engaged in ethnic cleansing, or *geno-cide*, to rid their country of an unwanted group or minority. Lawyer Raphael Lemkin connected Greek prefix *genos*, meaning race, to Latin suffix *-cide*, meaning killing, to describe what the Nazis did to the Jews during World War II. The United Nations declared genocide a crime under international law on December 11, 1946. Nearly two years later, on December 9, 1948, parties adopted the Convention on the Prevention and Punishment of the Crime of Genocide, which Lemkin initiated, and opened it for signature.

The convention defines genocide as killing members of a group, injuring members of a group physically or mentally, preventing births within a group via fertilization, forced abortion, or any other means, transferring children from the targeted group to another group, or deliberately inflicting conditions that will cause a group's physical destruction with the intent to destroy, in whole or in part, a national, ethnical, racial, or religious group. Punishable offenses include attempting to commit genocide, committing genocide, conspiring to commit genocide, inciting the public to commit genocide, and helping others commit genocide.

Since then, there have been several conflicts that have been defined as genocide under the UN convention. In the late 1970s, Cambodia was ruled by a communist group known as the Khmer Rouge. The group's leader, Pol Pot, wanted to trans-

Dr. Raphael Lemkin, who coined the word "genocide," also helped to draft the UN Genocide Convention in 1948. This international legislation was intended to prevent and punish the crime of genocide—the mass destruction of national, ethnic, racial, or religious groups.

form the country into a communist peasant farming society. He declared that Cambodia had to be purified of all foreign influences, including urban life, business, and religion. He forcibly transported Cambodians from cities to the countryside, and put them to work on farms. Between 1975 and 1979, approximately two million Cambodians—about one-quarter of the country's total population—died due to the Khmer Rouge policies. Many Cambodians fled the country as refugees, seeking safe haven in neighboring countries like Thailand.

In 1994, members of the Hutu ethnic group in the African country of Rwanda began attacking members of another ethnic group, the Tutsi. Hutu militias, armed with machetes, clubs, guns, and grenades, roamed around slaughtering Tutsi *civilians*. All Rwandans carried identification cards specifying their tribe, and these cards were now being used to determine whether a person should live or die. The United Nations sent peacekeeping troops, but withdrew them after ten Belgian soldiers were tortured and murdered by Hutus. However, no effort was made to evacuate or protect Tutsi civilians. The killings were only halted in July 1994 when Tutsis from neighboring countries invaded Rwanda and defeated the Hutu extremists. By then, around 800,000 people had been killed. The flow of refugees from Rwanda destabilized neighboring countries and contributed to *civil wars* and fighting in the Congo and other places throughout the 1990s.

During the 1990s, the country of Yugoslavia experienced a terrible breakup. Yugoslavia had been created shortly after World War I ended in 1918, by uniting several provinces in southeastern Europe where Slavic peoples lived. However, by the late 1980s tensions were beginning to show among Yugoslavia's different ethnic and religious groups. Civil war broke out in Yugoslavia during 1991, and the country began to fall apart.

Slobodan Milosevic, president of the Serbian Republic, saw an opportunity to create a "Greater Serbia" that would be open to all of the ethnic Serbs from Yugoslavia. Milosevic wanted Serbia to take control of another former Yugoslavian province, Bosnia and Herzegovenia. Most of Bosnia's population was Muslim, although it had a large Serbian minority who wished to remain part of Yugoslavia. Milosevic ordered the national army of Yugoslavia, which was dominated by Serbs, to attack Sarajevo, Bosnia's capital city. Serb snipers terrorized the city by shooting down civilians in the streets. There were many casualties, including 3,500 children.

The Bosnian Muslims were no match for the Yugoslav army, and the Serbs gradually took control of the region. As each town was captured, they rounded up the local Muslim population and either imprisoned them in *concentration camps* or; in some cases, massacred them. Women and girls were frequently the victims of rape. The plan was to turn Bosnia into a purely Serbian province. The process became known as "ethnic cleansing."

Western powers like the United States and Great Britain tried through diplomatic means to bring the fighting to an end. Safe havens were established by the United Nations, but these were ignored by the Serbs. In one safe haven, at Srebrenica, a Serbian force rounded up 7,500 Muslim men and boys between the ages of 12 and 60, and slaughtered them in July 1995.

The North Atlantic Treaty Organization (NATO), an international organization established in 1949 by the United States and countries of western Europe to promote international defense and collective security, responded by launching a major bombing campaign, attacking Serb positions throughout Bosnia. The Serbs found they had no choice but to negotiate. A peace deal was agreed to in 1995. By this time, however, 200,000 Muslims had been massacred; over 20,000 were missing, feared dead; and two million Muslims had become refugees.

The region known as Sudan, in northeastern Africa, has been plagued by civil war since the mid-1950s. The northern part of Sudan is predominantly Muslim in religion and Arab in ethnicity. Southern Sudan is home to black African tribes who practice either Christianity or traditional African religions.

A Bosnian Muslim prays over the grave of her son in a Sarajevo graveyard, 1993.

The two regions waged a civil war from 1955 until 1972 that led to more than 500,000 deaths. The conflict resumed in 1983 and lasted until 2003, when a cease-fire was signed after more than a million more Sudanese deaths. In 2011, the state was divided into two countries, Sudan and South Sudan.

At the same time, a conflict was occurring in the western part of Sudan that most experts characterized as genocide. The Darfur conflict began as a rivalry between farmers and herdsmen over pastureland. The farmers, many of whom were of African descent, attempted to prevent nomadic herdsmen of

An Indonesian member of a peacekeeping force patrols a refugee camp in the Darfur region of western Sudan.

Arab ethnicity, known as the Baggara, from grazing their flocks on land used for their crops. The Baggara responded by attacking villages and forcing out the farmers.

In 2003 two groups, the Justice and Equality Movement (JEM) and the Sudanese Liberation Army, rebelled against Sudan's government, claiming that it had sided with the Baggara by assisting an Arab militia called the *janjaweed*. Both sides were accused of significant human rights violations, including looting, rapes, mass killings, and the destruction of entire villages. In particular, the *janjaweed* was accused of carrying out a policy of "ethnic cleansing" in the Darfur region.

The African Union brokered a ceasefire in April 2004 and sent peacekeeping troops in to ensure compliance. However, the conflict continued, and by 2006 the United Nations estimated that over 400,000 people had been killed in Darfur, with another 2 million people driven from their homes. That year the UN proposed sending a larger peacekeeping force of more than 17,000 soldiers to replace the smaller African Union force. However, Sudan refused to allow the UN peacekeepers into the country. Instead, the government launched a major military offensive against the rebel groups.

During the years of fighting, there have been several ceasefire agreements in hopes of negotiating a peace. The most recent came in February 2010, when the Justice and Equality Movement agreed to talks with the Sudanese government. However, the talks have gone nowhere and sporadic violence by both sides has continued in the region.

War

On average, forty-two thousand and five hundred people fled their home each day of 2014, during the third year of the Syrian civil war, according to UNHCR's annual *Global Trends Report*.

"Evidently, armed conflict continues to be the biggest driver of displacement," UN High Commissioner for Refugees António Guterres told UNHCR's executive committee in

October 2015. "Fifteen new conflicts have broken out or reignited in the past five years, while none of the old ones got resolved."

From 2004 to 2014, the total number of refugees worldwide increased from 37.5 million to nearly 59.5 million.

Some wars, such as World War I and II, have been fought among different countries. Civil wars are fought largely within the borders of one nation, between those in power and those seeking power. Since World War II, civil wars have been fought on almost every continent. They often persist for years. For instance, the civil wars in Syria, Libya, and Iraq all began in 2011 and fighting in these conflicts continues today. Some wars, such as the Columbian conflict and the Somali civil war, have lasted decades.

Civil wars can start when a regional group fights not for total control of a country but for independence from the rest of the country. The 1991 break-up of the Soviet Union created a number of independent countries. When the people of Chechnya declared independence, the Russian Federation, of which Chechnya was a part, responded in 1994 by invading. Hundreds of thousands of people fled the country.

How Does War Create Refugees?

Since the civil war began in Syria in 2011, more than two hundred thousand people have been killed, more than twenty-eight thousand civilians have been executed, at least forty-nine children have been shot at close range, more than twenty-seven thousand civilians have died during bombings, nearly nineteen thousand people have been killed in barrel bomb attacks at

A Syrian Army tank near the entrance to the town of Ma'loula. In March 2016, US Secretary of State John Kerry declared that the atrocities committed by one of the factions fighting in Syria, the Islamic State of Iraq and the Levant (ISIL) amounted to genocide.

mosques, schools, and stores, nearly nine thousand civilians have been kidnapped or tortured by the government and the opposition, hundreds of people have been killed in chemical attacks using chlorine or sarin, nearly seven hundred hospital employees have been killed in three hundred attacks on medical facilities, and nearly six hundred people have died from starvation, dehydration, or preventable diseases, according to a September 2015 article in the *New York Times*. Considering statistics such as these, it's no wonder that Syrians are fleeing the country en masse.

"With each passing day there are fewer safe places in Syria," Paulo Sérgio Pinheiro, chairman of the United Nations panel investigating human rights abuses in Syria, wrote in a recent report. "Everyday decisions—whether to visit a neighbor, to go out to buy bread—have become, potentially, decisions about life and death."

What Are Human Rights?

After the atrocities that occurred in the concentration camps during World War II, the UN General Assembly adopted the Universal Declaration of Human Rights. The document "represents the universal recognition that basic rights and fundamental freedoms are inherent to all human beings, inalienable and equally applicable to everyone, and that every one of us is born free and equal in dignity in rights," according to the UN.

"Torture has long been used in Sri Lanka to persecute minorities, crush dissent, and stifle civil society," according to the organization Freedom From Torture (FFT). "It is deeply entrenched in the fabric of the state and has persisted across the decades regardless of changes in political leadership." In a report spanning 2009 to 2013, many people had been beaten, burned, stabbed, or suffocated with burning chili pepper or oil fumes. "Seventy-one percent of the cases in our study suffered some form of sexual violence as part of torture. Eighty-seven per cent of women and thirty percent of men were raped. Some women were raped night after night by different officers, while men also described being raped on multiple occasions. Almost half of the people in the study were forced to remain naked, causing them intense humiliation."

It would be a mistake to believe poor, developing countries are the only ones capable of committing human rights abuses, however. Nonprofit organization Human Rights Watch has criticized the United States for its use of solitary confinement. Others decry the death penalty. According to a Senate Intelligence Committee report, which has been called "the torture report," per NPR, the CIA committed a number of human rights abuses while interrogating Guantanamo Bay suspects in the years post-9/11.

 ## Text-Dependent Questions

1. What is the definition of genocide?
2. What causes the highest number of refugees?

 ## Research Project

Using the Internet or your school library, research the human rights that are included in the Universal Declaration of Human Rights. This document was adopted in 1948. Do you believe any rights should be added to or deleted from the list? Explain your answer in a two-page report and share it with your class.

Who Helps Refugees?

"The number of people uprooted from their homes by war and persecution in 2014 was larger than in any year since detailed record-keeping began," the *Washington Post* reported in June 2015. According to UNHCR's annual Global Trends report, the total number of refugees, asylum seekers, and internally displaced people increased from 37.5 million in 2004 to 59.5 million in 2014. As a means of comparison, California, the most populous state in the country, boasted 38.8 million residents in 2015. Great Britain boasted 63.8 million. Regardless of how you look at it, 59.5 million equates to a lot of people who need help.

High Commissioner for Refugees

It has been estimated that ten million people became refugees or internally displaced persons during World War I. When the

Workers with the United Nations High Commissioner for Refugees (UNHCR) register refugees on the Greek island of Kos. Many of the refugees are from Iraq, Syria, and Afghanistan, and they arrive at Kos on inflatable boats from Turkey.

war ended, the League of Nations, an international committee based on neutral ground in Geneva, Switzerland, and designed to prevent another war, set out to help those refugees. To do so, it appointed Chairman Fridtjof Nansen as High Commissioner for Refugees in 1921. Realizing that refugees' lack of identification papers created problems in their search for asylum, Nansen created the Nansen passport, which gave refugees with no identification papers the right to travel safely.

The Nansen International Office for Refugees, established after Nansen's death, was awarded the Nobel Peace Prize in 1938. "Nansen worked tirelessly on behalf of refugees, facing setbacks alongside the triumphs," according to UNHCR. "He was saddened by the evidence of human indifference to the suffering of others."

With that in mind, UNHCR created the Nansen Refugee Award in 1954 to recognize other *humanitarians* who help refugees.

What Does UNHCR Do?

Like the League of Nations, which was created after World War I to prevent another war, the United Nations, or UN, came

 Words to Understand in This Chapter

ambassador—highest-ranking diplomat.

humanitarian—a kind, charitable person who wants to help others.

policies—courses of action; strategies.

United Nations Secretary-General Ban Ki-moon (right) with Filippo Grandi, newly sworn-in UN High Commissioner for Refugees, January 2016.

together after World War II to resolve international conflicts peacefully and to establish *policies*. Five years after its foundation in 1945, the UN created a department called the Office of the United Nations High Commissioner for Refugees (UNHCR) to help those who'd been displaced during World War II.

The Office of the United Nations High Commissioner for Refugees was established on December 14, 1950, by the United Nations General Assembly. The following year, on July 28, the United Nations Convention Relating to the Status of

Officers from the UN High Commission for Refugees (UNHCR) unload tents in Djerba, Tunisia, to assist the hundreds fleeing across the border from Libya, where the government was launching deadly attacks against masses of civilian protesters, February 2011.

Refugees—the legal foundation of helping refugees and the basic statute guiding UNHCR's work—was adopted. This convention defined the term "refugee" and set forth a number of rights that refugees are entitled to. For instance, Article 7 states, "Except where this Convention contains more favorable provisions, a Contracting State shall accord to refugees the same treatment as is accorded to aliens generally." Another article provides the right to practice one's religion, which is important to those who've fled their homeland as a result of religious persecution.

UNHCR is also in charge of ensuring that ratifying parties uphold their obligations under the Convention Relating to the Status of Refugees.

Since its formation in 1950, UNHCR, in collaboration with governments and charities, has provided tents, food, clean drinking water, blankets, hygiene kits, legal assistance, transportation, grants, farming tools and seeds, home-building materials, school supplies, and medical care to more than 50 million displaced people.

UNHCR named actress Angelina Jolie Pitt a Goodwill *Ambassador* in 2001. Over the next decade, she donated more

In December 2015, UNHCR assisted in the voluntary repatriation of tens of thousands of refugees Côte d'Ivoire. The refugees had been living in neighboring Liberia for more than a year because of a deadly Ebola outbreak.

than five million dollars to fund schools in refugee camps in Kenya, Afghanistan, and other locations. She also worked to raise awareness of refugee issues. In 2005, Jolie Pitt started the National Center for Refugee and Immigrant Children, which provides free legal aid to young asylum seekers. Two years later, the International Rescue Committee, which former refugee Albert Einstein helped create in 1933, awarded a Freedom Award to both Jolie Pitt and UNHCR High Commissioner António Guterres for their work.

Today, the UNHCR has a number of goodwill ambassadors. They include Yao Chen, a Chinese actress and blogger; Julien Clerc, a French singer-songwriter; George Dalaras, a Greek musician; Muazzez Ersoy, a Turkish singer; Khaled Hosseini, an American author; Adel Imam, an Egyptian actor; Jung Woo-sung, a South Korean actor; Osvaldo Laport, a Uruguayan actor; Aidos Sagat, a composer/singer from Kazakhstan; Jesús Vázquez, a Spanish TV presenter; and Alek Wek, a British supermodel.

Other Organizations That Help Refugees

Many organizations, such as Amnesty International, campaign for human rights. Other charities help people who are suffering from homelessness, poverty, malnutrition, or ill health. Refugees often fall into one or more of these categories.

During the Syrian civil war, whitehouse.gov referred potential donors to International Medical Corps, International Rescue Committee, Mercy Corps, Save the Children, Concern Worldwide, World Renew, World Vision, CARE USA, World

Angelina Jolie Pitt (right), special envoy of the United Nations High Commissioner for Refugees (UNHCR), addresses a UN Security Council meeting on the conflict in Syria and the related humanitarian and refugee crises that have occurred as a result. At her side is António Guterres, a Portuguese diplomat who served as High Commissioner for Refugees from 2005 to 2015.

Food Programme USA (WFP), ShelterBox USA, and various faith-based charities, such as Church World Service, Catholic Relief Services, International Orthodox Christian Charities, Islamic Relief USA, Jesuit Refugee Service, and Lutheran World Relief. The list also included large, well-known organizations such as Oxfam and UNICEF, which provide healthcare, food, water, and shelter directly to emergency areas.

This truck was part of a UNHCR convoy carrying emergency shelter supplies for survivors of the cyclone Nargis in Myanmar.

The United Nations General Assembly created the United Nations Children's Emergency Fund (UNICEF) in 1946 to provide food and healthcare to children in World War II-ravaged countries. The organization continues to provide emergency relief and, one day during the Syrian civil war, turned over its Twitter account to four teens who fled to Turkey, Jordan, and Austria, so they could share their stories.

As the world becomes more connected via social media, people often start their own charities, so they can help one on one instead of donating to some faceless organization. For instance, during the Syrian civil war, a social worker, a woman who studied for her master's degree in religion and culture, and a communications design major in Berlin created Refugees Welcome. The Facebook page and website invite people in Germany, Austria, Greece, Portugal, Spain, Sweden, the Netherlands, and Poland to share their home with refugees the way people have opened up their home to travellers for years.

"Housing refugees in private accommodation brings advantages for both sides," the website said. "Refugees are able to live in adequate accommodation, learn the language better, and adjust to the new environment more easily. You, on the other hand, will get to know a different culture and help a person in a difficult situation."

Once someone signs up and answers a few questions about how many people already live in the home, what languages are spoken, and details about the city and neighborhood, Refugees Welcome connects the person to a local, external refugee organization, which finds a suitable refugee and arranges a meeting between the two parties. If they like one another, the refugee moves in, and the host is welcome to contact Refugees Welcome or the refugee organization with any questions or concerns. As of October 2015, Refugees Welcome had matched two hundred and seventy refugees with homes.

How Does the United States Help Refugees?

The United States donates the most money to humanitarian aid. From 2011 to 2015 alone, the U.S. spent $4.5 billion to help charitable organizations provide food, water, basic necessities, and healthcare during the Syrian civil war, per whitehouse.gov.

The U.S. also takes in "more refugees than every other country in the world combined," according to Kathleen Newland, who co-founded the Migration Policy Institute and spoke with *The Atlantic* in September 2015. In 2014, the U.S. accepted 70,000 refugees, including close to 2,000 from Syria.

"President Obama has directed his Administration to scale up the number of Syrian refugees we will bring to the U.S. next year to ten thousand," the White House said.

Why Doesn't the United States Take in More Refugees?

The United States has accepted less than two thousand Syrian refugees during the country's four-year civil war. Germany will take in 800,000 during 2015. Of course, Germany is a lot closer to Syria, but there are other reasons for the disparity.

First, three-quarters of the applications come as referrals from UNHCR. The organization did not begin sending applications en masse until June 2014, when it began referring between five hundred and one thousand people per month, according to *The Atlantic* magazine.

Second, the application-to-admission process takes between eighteen and twenty-four months. A State Department spokesperson told the *Washington Post* that refugees undergo more scrutiny than anyone else entering the country.

"That screening includes health checks, repeated biometric verification of identity, several layers of biographical and background screening, and in-person interviews. Multiple agencies are involved in the process, including the FBI's Terrorist

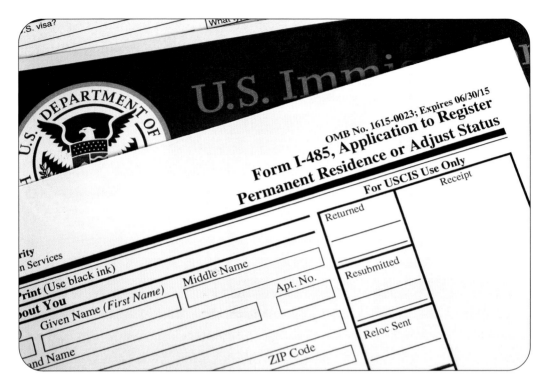

The US Department of Homeland Security is responsible for screening those who apply for asylum in the United States. Since 1975, Americans have welcomed over 3 million refugees from all over the world.

Screening Center, the State Department, the Department of Homeland Security, the National Counterterrorism Center, and the Department of Defense," the spokesperson said.

Still, people have voiced concerns. In response to a May 2015 letter in which fourteen U.S. Senate Democrats asked the Obama administration to allow 65,000 Syrian refugees into the country, Republican Representative Michael McCaul wrote his own letter.

"While we have a proud history of welcoming refugees, the Syrian conflict is a unique case requiring heightened vigilance and scrutiny," McCaul, whose Homeland Security Committee has held hearings on the issue, said. "It represents the single largest convergence of Islamist terrorists in history." Republican Representative Peter King of New York agreed.

Other Governments' Reluctance to Help

The 1951 Convention Relating to the Status of Refugees says countries should help refugees, but it does not force them to. Unfortunately, some people take the stance that charity should begin at home, meaning countries should dedicate money and resources to their own country's problems. Thus, some governments choose not to grant asylum to those who seek it. Others try to force refugees to return to their home country.

In 2001, Australian Prime Minister John Howard prevented a ship carrying more than four hundred asylum seekers predominantly from Afghanistan from arriving in Australia. He signed a deal to take them elsewhere, and his popularity swelled, per BBC News.

Many of the world's governments are democratically elected, meaning politicians are voted in by people during elections. Consequently, politicians try to make decisions that are popular with the voting public, so they will be re-elected. As mentioned earlier regarding Australians' view of asylum seekers, in many countries, a large percentage of the population dislikes or fears refugees. As a result, politicians sometimes see helping refugees and asylum seekers as a "vote loser."

Wealthy, industrialized countries donate millions of dollars in aid, but critics argue that they could do a lot more to help nations struggling with huge numbers of refugees. For instance, Amnesty International and Human Rights Watch called out Qatar, United Arab Emirates, Saudi Arabia, Kuwait, Oman, and Bahrain in September 2015 for refusing to take in a single Syrian refugee as Europe dealt with a flood of them.

"These countries include some of the Arab world's largest military budgets, its highest standards of living, as well as a lengthy history—especially in the case of the United Arab Emirates—of welcoming immigrants from other Arab nations and turning them into citizens," a Dubai-based political commentator told the *Washington Post*.

But, like other countries, these Gulf states have the same fears about security, terrorism, and refugees taking citizens' jobs, the article stated.

 # Text-Dependent Questions

1. Who created passports for refugees?
2. How do charitable organizations help refugees?

 # Research Project

Using the Internet or your school library, research charitable organizations and write a two-page report on whether they truly help or whether they merely act as a Band-Aid. A response in favor of charities may argue that charities raise millions of dollars, bring relief to many refugees, and raise awareness about their plight. A response against charities may argue that despite all the money they have raised, the refugee problem remains. Why has it never been solved? Governments might do more if charities did less.

4

What Happens to Refugees?

Refugees are often forced to say goodbye to all that they know as a sudden decision made amid fear and chaos. What follows is rarely easy or straightforward. Fleeing to safety can involve great hardship, suffering, and even death. To become a refugee, you have to escape your immediate area, reach and cross your country's border, and find refuge on the other side.

Most people who flee their homeland travel on foot and seek shelter along the way. Their journey is often dangerous due to natural hazards. In tropical regions, people in flight risk death from the heat, as well as lack of food or water. In contrast, people fleeing parts of Albania and Chechnya in winter have had to contend with bitter cold and the dangers of pneumonia and hypothermia. People in flight also sometimes have

Hungarian police keep order as Syrian refugees arrive at the Gyekenyes Zakany Railway Station. Throughout 2015 and 2016, refugees were arriving constantly in Hungary on their way to Germany.

to deal with human hazards, such as straying into areas of military action or being attacked and robbed. Some war-torn countries, such as Sudan, Angola, Cambodia, Croatia, Iraq, and Nicaragua, are peppered with unmarked land mines. In 2012, North Korea cracked down on border crossings by planting land mines and telling border guards they were allowed to shoot to kill.

People in flight face the ever-present fear of being caught and returned home, where they may be imprisoned or executed. During the refugee crisis in Mozambique, South African border authorities caught nearly two thousand people per month and forced them to return to their home country.

What Is People Trafficking?

Refugees often turn to people *smugglers* to help them escape their country. For instance, eighteen Sri Lankan refugees sold all of their belongings and paid a Bulgarian trucker $800 to

 Words to Understand in This Chapter

cholera—an infectious and often fatal bacterial disease of the small intestine, typically contracted from infected water supplies and causing severe vomiting and diarrhea.

dysentery—intestinal inflammation that causes bloody diarrhea.

non-refoulement—a principle of international law that forbids true victims of persecution to be returned to their persecutor.

repatriated—sent back to one's own country.

smugglers—people who import or export goods or other people secretly, in violation of the law.

Often, refugees must wait for the right time to cross a nation's borders, or receive help from smugglers that they pay to help them escape from their homelands.

transport them to Germany and Italy. The truck's ventilation system broke down soon after they left, and the refugees had no way to escape, since the trailer had been locked from the outside.

The grisly sight of their decomposing bodies found locked inside the refrigerated trailer of a truck has been embedded in the mind of UNHCR deputy representative Ditlev Nordgaard in Budapest, Hungary, according to *Refugees Magazine*. "It was a terrible tragedy," Nordgaard said. "You could hardly recognize the faces."

In many countries, people trafficking has grown into a network involving corrupt border officials, who are bribed.

In North Korea, Melanie Kirkpatrick said in *Escape from North Korea: The Untold Story of Asia's Underground Railroad*, "Brokers are a necessary evil." Women who try to cross the border without the aid of a legitimate broker may be caught in China and sold into sex slavery or marriage. If returned home, or *repatriated*, they may suffer an even worse fate.

According to Kirkpatrick, "North Korea forces repatriated women to have abortions, even in the final months of pregnancy, and it kills newborns it believes have Chinese fathers."

What Is Enforced Repatriation?

Enforced repatriation means sending refugees home against their will. The 1951 UN Convention protects refugees from enforced repatriation if they are likely to face persecution. This protection is called *non-refoulement*. For asylum seekers whose application fails, there is no such protection. After all avenues of appeal have failed, asylum seekers are often sent home.

"It is widely accepted that the prohibition of forcible return is part of customary international law," UNHCR stated in its Guide to International Refugee Law. "This means that even States that are not party to the 1951 Refugee Convention must respect the principle of non-refoulement."

Who Were the "Boat People?"

After South Vietnam fell under communist control in April 1975, tens of thousands of people began fleeing the country by boat each month, Vinh Chung wrote in *Where the Wind Leads*.

Refugees from Cambodia, Vietnam and Laos in their living quarters in a camp in Bangkok, Thailand, July 1979. The refugees from war-torn Southeast Asia were mostly resettled in the United States, Canada, Italy, and France.

"[O]f every two refugees who left Vietnam, only one survived."

Chung's family left in 1979, a couple of years after the government took over their multimillion dollar rice empire, their house, their cars, their motorcycle, and everything else they owned, and after Vietnam went to war with China. Viet Cong sympathizers had made the Chungs' lives increasingly difficult and, with eight children facing starvation, they had no choice but to flee.

The border to China had been sealed shut, so they decided to buy a boat rather than risk life and limb trekking through the Cambodia's killing fields or Laos' land mines. They left their farm in small groups to avoid raising suspicion.

"First, we travelled from the farm to Bac Lieu, which we hoped would look like nothing more than a regular visit to my mother's family home," Chung wrote. "From Bac Lieu we travelled by bus in the direction of Ca Mau [a well-known port that many refugees had fled from], but we took the precaution of stopping halfway there in case anyone on the bus recognized us; we even spent the night in a temple instead of staying with friends to avoid starting any rumors about our plans." The trip from the farm to the port should have taken two hours; instead, it took three days.

The government had long since started charging people to leave the country, so a Public Security Bureau agent met them on the dock.

"It was evening by the time everyone was on board and ready to depart. There were no seats or benches on the boat, so we all sat cross-legged on the rough wooden decks and squeezed in as tightly as possible to make room for everyone," Chung wrote. "Before the boat even left the dock, the passengers below deck had already begun complaining. They were packed together like cattle and forced to share what little space they had with the baggage, food, and fuel."

Worse, nearly three hundred people were crammed onto a boat with no bathroom. When people below deck became seasick, they passed their vomit to the upper deck in buckets, so it could be tossed overboard.

Somewhere in the South China Sea en route to Malaysia, fifteen pirates boarded the boat and robbed the passengers.

"The men on our boat did nothing because they didn't dare," Chung wrote. "It wasn't what did happen that paralyzed them with fear; it was the thought of what could happen. That fear is something all refugees experience because refugees are forced to sail across pirate waters all their lives. So many things can go wrong for a refugee, but it's the fear of what could go wrong that haunts us."

After three days of beautiful weather, someone spotted land. As the boat drew closer, people onshore began yelling at them to turn around. Passengers gouged the hull with metal, so

Refugees from Cambodia, Vietnam, and Laos are processed at a camp in Thailand, 1979.

Vietnamese refugees in Thailand wait for resettlement in the United States, 1979.

the boat would take on water, and the people onshore would have to let them stay.

More than three hundred thousand Vietnamese refugees had fled to Malaysia, Indonesia, Singapore, Thailand, and the Philippines in the previous four years. Malaysia had taken in more than one hundred and twenty thousand, but their hospitality had worn thin.

"[Refugees'] sheer numbers began to overwhelm the job market and social services of the country," Chung said. "Ordinary Malaysians like these villagers had borne the brunt of it because they were the ones competing for those jobs and social services. By the time our family arrived in Malaysia, the nation was suffering from what some have called 'compassion fatigue,' and our beach reception committee wanted to make it very clear that our kind were no longer welcome there."

That "committee" forced the new arrivals to march the perimeter of the island for five days. During that time, Chung's mother suffered a miscarriage, hemorrhaged, and nearly bled out before a group of villagers took her to the hospital. No one in Chung's family was allowed to go with her. They weren't sure they would see her again.

By the time she rejoined the group, another refugee boat had arrived and been forced to march. The villagers conned all of the refugees onto tiny boats tied behind a ship, believing they were being transported to a refugee camp on an island a couple of hours away.

Twenty hours later, the villagers cut the ropes, said, "You're on your own now," and left the refugees, directionless, in the middle of the sea.

After five days of starvation and dehydration, Stan Mooneyham saved them.

Mooneyham, a Christian who served as president of a charity called World Vision, started Operation Seasweep after seeing news reports about the boat people who'd died. Congressmen and State Department officials had cautioned him not to do anything, but he remained undeterred. He toured Southeast Asia refugee camps and a cargo ship packed with refugees, and conferred with six government officials who refused to help.

Discouraged, he rode to the hotel with a colleague who came up with the idea of providing refugee ships with food, water, and other necessities, including ship repairs.

"They didn't have to rescue the refugees," Chung wrote. "They could just resupply them. And why not? That was exactly what World Vision was doing for the poor and hungry all over the world—they didn't remove people from their desperate situations; they just provided assistance for them while they were there."

Ultimately, a Lutheran church in Arkansas sponsored Chung's family and provided them with a house for six months. Chung played football in high school, went to his prom, graduated from Harvard Medical School, got married, and had four children. But other boat people are still fleeing for their lives.

Life in a Refugee Camp

Some refugees sneak over the border and "disappear" into a new country, living on the move or going into hiding. The majority arrive at relief or transit camps and then move on to refugee camps.

Life in a refugee camp can be disorienting and traumatic as refugees try to adjust to a new way of life and suffer nightmares. Camps in Darfur set up schools, believing a routine would help children adjust.

Despite the best efforts of aid workers and local people, conditions in refugee camps can be appalling. Many refugees arrive ill or injured. With limited medical facilities and often poor sanitation in camps, the risk of disease and infection runs

This refugee camp in France is a muddy camp with a lot of dirty waste. People are cold and hungry.

high. For example, in July 1994, when one million Rwandan refugees poured into eastern Zaire over four days, more than fifty thousand people died of *cholera*, *dysentery*, and other diseases. Measles, diarrhea, acute respiratory infections, and malaria cause more than sixty percent of deaths. Children often suffer malnutrition when camps run low on aid or when children refuse to eat food they aren't accustomed to.

Aid workers helping Darfur genocide survivors recognized a need for social and psychological support.

"As soon as an injustice or inequality appears in the camp,

Medical professionals with the Red Crescent examine a Somalian woman in the Dadaab refugee camp in Kenya, 2011.

it sparks a fire," a CARE worker told documentary filmmakers. "Any imbalance can bring out a lot of repressed feeling: anger, dissatisfaction, frustration, and grief. People start to fight with wood sticks over little incidents sometimes, and they hurt themselves for something that could be settled otherwise. It takes very little to reveal the hurt they've been through."

Brawls have broken out in tented German refugee camps during the Syrian civil war, according to *Newsweek*. Fourteen people, including three police officers, were injured in one camp housing fifteen hundred refugees from twenty different countries. "It is unclear what prompted the violence," *Newsweek* said.

In another camp, two Red Cross workers were injured after a teenage Afghan boy threatened a Syrian girl with a knife, sparking two hundred refugees to fight each other with bars, table legs, and bed frames.

How Long Do Refugee Camps Last?

Refugee camps are supposed to be a temporary safety net, but some refugee camps have lasted for decades.

Somalian children reach for food in the Dadaab refugee camp.

In the early 1990s, a civil war in Somalia sent more than three hundred and thirty thousand people fleeing to a refugee camp in Dadaab, Kenya, that was designed to house ninety thousand. In 2011, that camp turned twenty years old.

"Three generations of Palestinians displaced by the founding of Israel in 1948 know only life in U.N. refugee camps, going to schools beneath the blue-and-white U.N. flag and drawing their food stocks from U.N. warehouses," Reuters reported in 2012. About seven hundred thousand Palestinians fled their homes after the 1948 war, but nearly five million refugees and their children now live in camps in Lebanon, Syria, Jordan, the Gaza Strip and the West Bank. "For these Palestinians whose long-cherished goal is 'right of return' to the lands they lost 64 years ago, the camps must be seen as temporary no matter how permanent they might seem to others."

The longer refugees remain in a camp, the greater the potential for them to become dependent upon aid, relying on the assistance of others to live. Children can grow into adults knowing no other way of living.

"We hope one day to be done with dependence," one man told reporters. "Everybody should depend on himself."

The Dangers of Refugee Camps

Most refugee camps are located in neighboring countries. Sometimes, such as in Africa, these are poor, developing countries which can barely feed, clothe, and shelter their own people, much less an influx of refugees. In other cases, because the camps are located on borders they are vulnerable to attack.

However, even camps far away from the fighting are sometimes vulnerable. A hostel in Sweden that was going to house sixty Syrian refugees was burned to the ground in October 2015. More than two hundred camps for Syrian refugees have been attacked in Germany, which has taken in the highest number of refugees during the Syrian civil war. In August 2015, an arsonist burned down a shelter near Berlin.

 # Text-Dependent Questions

1. Who helps North Koreans cross the border to escape the country?
2. Why did writer Vinh Chung and his family flee Vietnam?

 # Research Project

Do you think refugees should be allowed to stay in camps indefinitely, or do you believe there should be a time limit? Write a two-page report summarizing your response. An argument in favor of allowing refugees to stay as long as they want may say semi-permanent camps could be built with proper facilities, so people could remain safely in one place until the conflict in their country ends. An argument against allowing refugees to stay as long as they want may say semi-permanent camps would increase dependency upon aid, diminish refugees' hope of returning home, and increase resentment among the host country's citizens.

Problems That Refugees Face

Most refugees arrive in a new country with few possessions but plenty of terrible experiences seared into their memory. Making a fresh start in a new country is rarely the end of a refugee's struggles. In fact, camps present a number of challenges.

First, refugees have to worry about being accepted by a host country that may see them as a threat to resources, jobs, and social services. After making the difficult decision to abandon family, friends, and everything they own in order to flee persecution in one country, they may encounter discrimination, including verbal abuse and violence, in another.

Second, refugees may be lumped into a camp with members of the group that persecuted them in their homeland. This may cause conflict. Sometimes, such as International Rescue

◀————————————————————

A Syrian police officer patrols along the fence around a refugee camp on the border between Syria and Turkey. The UNHCR reported in 2016 that there were more refugees worldwide than at any time since the end of World War II.

Committee's observations of the Rohingya tribe, refugees remain in dark, suffocating quarters because they're afraid to open their windows.

However they are distributed, refugees usually find themselves relegated to a *ghetto* in a poor part of town. If the camp lies on the outskirts, it may be attacked. Makeshift camps in squalid conditions often lead to bacterial, viral, and parasitic infections, since food shortages, poor sanitation, and unsafe drinking water are common. "We have high rates of mortality, above the emergency threshold plus high rates of malnutrition," one UNHCR employee told reporters about a Syrian refugee camp in 2012.

While dealing with all of these concerns, psychological trauma, and, if fleeing a war, injuries or disfigurement, refugees also have to acclimate to a new culture.

Language Barriers

The majority of refugees accepted into the U.S. come from Iraq, Iran, Burma, Bhutan, Somalia, Cuba, Democratic Republic of

 Words to Understand in This Chapter

exploitation—the act of treating someone unfairly in order to benefit from their work; abuse.

ghetto—a part of a city, especially a slum area, that is occupied by a minority group or groups.

scapegoat—a person who is blamed for the wrongdoings, mistakes, or faults of others.

When countries agree to accept refugees, some citizens are anxious that the newcomers may have a negative effect on their society, customs, and traditions. They may believe that refugees will bring the problems of their home countries, such as crime or disease. These Austrians are protesting against the construction of refugee shelters in Graz.

Residents of the Netherlands demonstrate against racism and Islamophobia at a February 2016 event in Amsterdam titled "Refugees welcome, racism not!"

Congo, and Eritrea, according to the Cultural Orientation Resource Center in 2010. Somalia and Enitrea are the only two that list English as a spoken language, per the Central Intelligence Agency's World Factbook.

It's difficult to communicate needs or find a job if you can't speak the language. Surveys in the U.S. and Southeast Asia have shown that refugees who speak the host country's language are twice as likely to find work and far more likely to land higher-paid jobs. For this reason, host countries, such as Sweden, grant free language tuition.

Even with assistance, it can be difficult for adults to learn a new language, however. Older generations tend to rely on children, who are quick learners, to be their interpreters.

Highly-educated refugees who work in professions or trades may already speak their host country's language, but, as mentioned earlier regarding North Korean doctors needing to be retrained before they can practice medicine in South Korea, they often have to retrain before they can work in their chosen field — if they're given the opportunity at all. In the meantime, refugees have to take whatever jobs they're given, which often means working in low-paid industries, where there is potential for *exploitation*.

An Iraqi girl at the refugee camp in Idomeni, Greece, March 2016.

Stranded refugees waiting to obtain support and medical care at the Keleti Palyudvar train station in Budapest, Hungary, September 2015.

Other Obstacles

Some refugees move to a new continent in order to seek sanctuary. This requires adjusting to a change in climate. It also means adapting to a new culture, including arts, music, and cuisine. The food that a refugee is accustomed to eating may not be available in his or her new country, or it may be too expensive.

Refugees may be accepted into a new country officially, but they are not always welcomed. Refugees are often placed in areas where the poorest people live. Their arrival can upset local people in need, especially if social services appear to favor the refugees. In times of economic difficulties, this resentment can lead to discrimination and abuse. Racists often turn refugees into *scapegoats* and blame them for all of their country's problems. As a result, many refugees live in fear of racist attacks.

Can Refugees Ever Truly Resettle?

Many people believe that refugees can never truly settle in their host country. They point to news stories about refugees wanting to return home, crimes they've committed, and complaints about their host country and the treatment they've received. But there are thousands of refugees who've not only settled but made outstanding contributions to their new country. Canada's first foreign-born Governor-General, Adrienne Clarkson, was a refugee forced to flee from Hong Kong during World War II. Successful British internet businessman Sieng Van Tran was one of the Vietnamese boat people in the 1970s. Carlos Eire, one of fourteen thousand children exiled from

Cuba without their parents in the 1960s, became a professor of history and religion at Yale and has written two memoirs about his experiences as a refugee in Miami. Several refugees have become Nobel Prize winners. And for every famous refugee, there are hundreds more who have benefitted their local community.

Some people see refugees as victims: people in need who are a drain on resources. Others look at refugees as remarkable people who have survived by virtue of their courage, persistence, and ingenuity — qualities valued in most countries. The challenge for governments is finding a way to integrate refugees into their societies.

Do Refugees Ever Return Home?

Nearly one hundred and thirty thousand people returned home in 2014, according to UNHCR's *Global Trends Report*. It may seem implausible that refugees would want to return home, especially while a war continues, but many do.

In October 2015, BBC News reported that more than one hundred Syrians were returning to their country each day, even though bombs continue to be dropped. Many had run out of money in their host country.

Eighty-six percent of Syrian refugees living in Jordan fell below the country's poverty line of ninety-six dollars per month. The government forbids them from working and does not provide food vouchers or healthcare, so many refugees saw no choice but to return home.

"It's a hard life here," said one man, who decided to stay in Jordan to take care of his elderly mother while his wife moved back to Syria with their child. "My baby daughter is really sick, and I can't afford her treatment. In Syria, it will be available."

Returning home can be as difficult for refugees as settling in a new country. Their experiences have altered their lives in a dramatic way, and they have to try to deal with the trauma they have been through. The happiness of being reunited with friends and family may be mixed with grief for relatives who have been killed since the refugees fled.

 Text-Dependent Questions

1. Why is it difficult for refugees to settle into their host country?
2. Why did Syrians return home during the civil war?

 Research Project

Using the Internet or your school library, research the obstacles refugees face when they arrive in a new country. Now imagine that you are a refugee who's fled your home country and that you had to abandon your friends, your pets, and everything you owned. Brainstorm ways that aid organizations and a host country's citizens could help you feel more at home and less scared. Write a two-page report and share it with your class.

Appendix

Refugees in Historical Context

T he term "refugee" was first used more than three hundred years ago to describe a group of people in France known as the Huguenots, who were Protestant. King Louis XIV was a Roman Catholic who saw the Huguenots as a threat to his throne and tried to coerce them into converting to Catholicism. When that failed, he began executing them and sentencing Protestant ministers and church attendees to prison for life. Between the late seventeenth century and the early eighteenth century, nearly one-fifth of France's population fled the country for non-Catholic parts of Europe, such as the Netherlands, Germany, Prussia, Switzerland, and Scandinavia. When they arrived in England, they were called "refugees," from the French verb *réfugier*, meaning "to take refuge."

Refugees existed long before the word was first used, however. People have been driven from their homes due to war,

Torture of Huguenots in France after the revocation of the Edict of Nantes, 1685.

This illustration shows Russian refugees fleeing a battlefield. The problem of refugees and displaced peoples has existed as long as humans have.

famine, and other problems throughout human history.

Refugees abound in the histories of the world's major religions. According to the Bible, the forebears of the Jewish people left their homeland due to a famine and settled in Egypt. After hundreds of years, the Egyptians pressed these people, known as the Israelites, into slavery. A leader named Moses eventually led them out of Egypt and back to their homeland. Followers of the Christian faith believe that Jesus Christ was taken as an infant to Egypt, so he could escape the persecution of children commanded by King Herod, the ruler of Judea at the time. Six centuries later, the Prophet Muhammad, the founder of Islam, fled the oppression of his home city, Mecca, with a small band of followers. They journeyed to another nearby village, Yathrib (later called Medina), where they established a Muslim community. This flight to safety in 622 CE, known as the Hegira, is commemorated by Muslims to this day and marks the starting point of their calendar.

Beginning in the sixteenth century, European countries explored other lands and claimed them as their colonies. Colonial powers—such as the French, Dutch, British, Spanish, and Portuguese—divided the continents among them. In doing

These Spanish soldiers who had supported the Republican side during that country's civil war are in a refugee camp at Boulou, France, in 1939.

Armenian families in a refugee camp, circa 1920. During the First World War, Armenians and other minorities in the Ottoman Empire were the targets of genocidal attacks.

so, especially in Africa, they ignored tribal and ethnic boundaries that had existed before their arrival. Consequently, territorial borders marked out for the convenience of the European countries began to create conflict and continue to do so today.

Prior to the start of World War I in 1914, people had more freedom to travel to other countries. After the war began, countries closed their borders to foreigners. A system of passports and visas was developed. Refugees found that they had nowhere to go, and this became a serious problem.

Another twentieth century development was the increase in the number of refugees created due to people being persecuted, tortured, and threatened with death because of their political opinions. Around 1.5 million opponents of communism left Russia between the start of the Russian Revolution in 1917 and the end of the civil war in 1921. During the Spanish Civil War from 1936 to 1939, 500,000 people were killed and 500,000 republicans fled to France. After World War II, somewhere between 30 and 50 million refugees had to be resettled between 1945 and 1948.

Famous Refugees

After the Nazi Third Reich accused German Jew Albert Einstein of treason in 1933, the physicist fled to the United States, where he accepted a position at Princeton University. Likewise, Austrian Sigmund Freud, who created psychoanalysis, fled to London in 1938 when the Nazis took over Austria, and the Gestapo arrested his daughter, Anna. She was ultimately allowed to return home, but the 82-year-old neurologist, who had jaw cancer, boarded a train and left.

The famous Austrian neurologist Sigmund Freud, known as the father of psychoanalysis, was a refugee from the Nazi regime in the 1930s.

Some young German Jews who fled Nazi persecution in the 1930s would grow up to become important American statesmen. The family of

Former refugee Madeleine Albright is awarded the Presidential Medal of Freedom by President Barack Obama in a 2012 ceremony at the White House.

Henry Kissinger moved to London, and later to New York. Kissinger would serve as US Secretary of State to presidents Nixon and Ford during the 1970s. Madeleine Albright, who in 1997 would become the first woman to serve as Secretary of States, fled with her family from Czechoslovakia when the Nazis gained control of the country.

"My father had been in the Czechoslovakian Diplomatic Service," Albright later recalled in a video for humanitarian aid group International Rescue Committee. "I was a refugee during World War II in England as a little girl and lived through the Blitz. I then went back and had a fairly glorious life as a daughter of an ambassador. And then all of a sudden we were again refugees, and came to the United States with nothing. We arrived on the East Coast but then ended up in Denver. And people were so terribly nice and you know provided us with furniture and Christmas presents. And it made me realize how grateful a refugee is and how important it is to be able to fit into some other communities."

Other refugees, such as actress Marlene Dietrich, Chilean novelist Isabel Allende, writer Anne Frank, and singer, musician, and songwriter Bob Marley have made important contributions to the arts in the United States.

In 1959, the spiritual and political leader of Tibet, the Dalai Lama Tenzin Gyatso, became a refugee due to an invasion from China. According to *Time* magazine, he disguised himself as a soldier during political protests and climbed the Himalayan mountains at night until he arrived in India two to three weeks later.

The exiled Buddhist leader was awarded the Nobel Peace Prize in 1989 for leading 40 years of nonviolent resistance as "an attempt both to influence events in China and to recognize

Dalai Lama Tenzin Gyatso speaks at a conference in Spain.

the efforts of student leaders of the democracy movement," friends of Nobel committee members told the *New York Times*.

Other Nobel Prize-Winning Refugees

Perhaps not surprisingly, refugees often go on to help other people. For instance, a number of refugees have won the Nobel Prize for their contributions to science and medicine. Physician and biochemist Sir Hans Adolf Krebs fled Germany for England when Hitler took power in 1933. Twenty years later, he won the Nobel Prize in Physiology or Medicine. Physicist and mathematician Max Born, who likewise emigrated to Britain in 1933 when the Nazis took power in Germany

Rigoberta Menchú, a Guatemalan indigenous leader, human rights activist, and Nobel Laureate speaks to the United Nations in 2014.

and suspended his work, won the 1954 Nobel Prize in Physics for his quantum mechanics research. Sir Bernard Katz, a Jew born in Germany, was awarded the 1970 Nobel Prize in Physiology or Medicine 35 years after fleeing to Britain during Hitler's reign. Physics professor Walter Kohn, who became separated from his parents while fleeing Austria in 1939, won the Nobel Prize for Chemistry in 1998.

Two former refugees have won the Nobel Prize in Literature since 1929. First, Paul Thomas Mann, a German writer who moved to Switzerland when Hitler took power in 1933 and moved to the United States when World War II broke out in 1939, was awarded the 1929 Nobel Prize in Literature for stories based on his family. Novelist and playwright Elias Canetti, who fled the Nazis and "spent much of his creative life analyzing the individual and the social and political forces that weighed against him in the 20th century," per the New York Times, won the Nobel Prize in Literature in 1981.

Writer, activist, and UNESCO Goodwill Ambassador Rigoberta Menchú, who escaped to Mexico during the Guatemalan Civil War in 1981, won the Nobel Peace Prize in 1992. Fourteen years later, she and five female Nobel Peace Prize winners created the Nobel Women's Initiative, which supports women's organizations that promote peace, justice, and equality.

Organizations to Contact

African Commission on Human and Peoples' Rights
31 Bijilo Annex Layout, Kombo North District
Western Region P.O. Box 673 Banjul
The Gambia
Phone: (220) 441 05 05
E-mail: au-banjul@africa-union.org
Website: http://www.achpr.org

American Refugee Committee
615 1st Ave NE, Suite 500
Minneapolis, MN 55413-2681
Phone: (800) 875-7060
Fax: (612) 607-6499
Email: Info@archq.org
Website: www.arcrelief.org/

Amnesty International
5 Penn Plaza
14th Floor
New York, NY 10001
Phone: (212) 807-8400
E-mail: aimember@aiusa.org
Website: http://www.amnestyusa.org

Canadian Council for Refugees

6839 Drolet #301

Montréal, Québec, H2S 2T1

Canada

Phone: (514) 277-7223

Fax: (514) 277-1447

E-mail: info@ccrweb.ca

Website: http://ccrweb.ca/en

CARE

151 Ellis Street, NE

Atlanta, GA 30303

Phone: 1-800-422-7385

E-mail: info@care.org

Website: www.care.org

European Council on Refugees and Exiles (ECRE)

Rue Royale 146, 1st Floor

1000 Brussels, Belgium

Phone: +32 (0)2 234 3800

Fax: +32 (0)2 514 5922

E-mail: ecre@ecre.org

Website: http://ecre.org/

Hand in Hand for Syria

47-49 Park Royal Road

London

NW10 7LQ

Website: http://handinhandforsyria.org.uk/

Human Rights Watch

350 Fifth Ave.

34th Floor

New York, NY 10118-3299

Phone: (212) 290-4700

E-mail: hrwnyc@hrw.org

Website: http://www.hrw.org

International Committee of the Red Cross (ICRC)

19 Avenue de la paix

CH 1202 Geneva

Phone: 41 22 734 60 01

Fax: 41 22 733 20 57

Website: http://icrc.org

Oxfam America

226 Causeway Street, 5th Floor

Boston, MA 02114-2206

Phone: (800) 77-OXFAM

Fax: (202) 496-1190

E-mail: info@oxfamamerica.org

Website: www.oxfamamerica.org

Refugee Council USA (RCUSA)

1628 16th St. NW

Washington, DC 20009

Phone: 202-319-2102

Fax: 202-319-2104

E-mail: info@rcusa.org

Website: http://rcusa.org

Refugees International
2001 S Street NW, Suite 700
Washington, DC 20009
Phone: 1-800-REFUGEE
Fax: 202.828.0819
E-mail: ri@refugeesinternational.org
Website: www.refugeesinternational.org

United Nations High Commissioner for Human Rights
Palais des Nations
CH-1211 Geneva 10
Switzerland
Phone: + 41 22 917 90 20
E-mail: InfoDesk@ohchr.org
Website: http://www.ohchr.org/english

**United Nations High Commissioner
for Refugees (UNHCR)**
Case Postale 2500
CH-1211 Geneva 2 Dépôt
Switzerland
Phone: 41 22 739 8111
Fax: 41 22 739 7377
Website: unhcr.org/

Series Glossary

apartheid—literally meaning "apartness," the political policies of the South African government from 1948 until the early 1990s designed to keep peoples segregated based on their color.

BCE and CE—alternatives to the traditional Western designation of calendar eras, which used the birth of Jesus as a dividing line. BCE stands for "Before the Common Era," and is equivalent to BC ("Before Christ"). Dates labeled CE, or "Common Era," are equivalent to *Anno Domini* (AD, or "the Year of Our Lord").

colony—a country or region ruled by another country.

democracy—a country in which the people can vote to choose those who govern them.

detention center—a place where people claiming asylum and refugee status are held while their case is investigated.

ethnic cleansing—an attempt to rid a country or region of a particular ethnic group. The term was first used to describe the attempt by Serb nationalists to rid Bosnia of Muslims.

house arrest—to be detained in your own home, rather than in prison, under the constant watch of police or other government forces, such as the army.

reformist—a person who wants to improve a country or an institution, such as the police force, by ridding it of abuses or faults.

republic—a country without a king or queen, such as the US.

United Nations—an international organization set up after the end of World War II to promote peace and co-operation throughout the world. Its predecessor was the League of Nations.

UN Security Council—the permanent committee of the United Nations that oversees its peacekeeping operations around the world.

World Bank—an international financial organization, connected to the United Nations. It is the largest source of financial aid to developing countries.

World War I—A war fought in Europe from 1914 to 1918, in which an alliance of nations that included Great Britain, France, Russia, Italy, and the United States defeated the alliance of Germany, Austria-Hungary, the Ottoman Empire, and Bulgaria.

World War II—A war fought in Europe, Africa, and Asia from 1939 to 1945, in which the Allied Powers (the United States, Great Britain, France, the Soviet Union, and China) worked together to defeat the Axis Powers (Germany, Italy, and Japan).

Further Reading

Alston, Philip, and Ryan Goodman. *International Human Rights*. New York: Oxford University Press, 2013.

Beeson, Mark, and Nick Bisley. *Issues in 21st Century World Politics*. New York: Palgrave Macmilan, 2013.

Chung, Vinh. *Where the Wind Leads*. Nashville: Thomas Nelson, 2014.

Eire, Carlos. *Learning to Die in Miami: Confessions of a Refugee Boy*. New York: Free Press, 2010.

Kirkpatrick, Melanie. *Escape from North Korea: The Untold Story of Asia's Underground Railroad*. New York: Encounter Books, 2012.

Linderman, Juliet. *Refugee Hotel*. San Francisco: McSweeney's, 2012.

Marlowe, Jen. *Darfur Diaries: Stories of Survival*. New York: Nation Books, 2006.

Sullivan, Anne Marie. *Syria*. Philadelphia: Mason Crest, 2015.

Internet Resources

https://www.amnesty.org/en/what-we-do/discrimination/
Amnesty International addresses discrimination worldwide with news, information on issues, initiatives for justice, and statistics.

www.exileimages.co.uk
A photo library devoted to pictures of refugees and development aid complete with photo case stories of refugees from all over the world.

www.hrw.org/refugees
The organization Human Rights Watch provides reports on human rights issues around the world. Each country also has its own page on this site.

www.refugeecamp.org
A graphic and informative look at refugee camps, including how they operate and the difficulties camp organizers and refugees face.

www.refugees.org
The home page of the U.S. Committee for Refugees and Immigrants has maps and background information on many regions generating refugees. Refugees' stories can be heard as sound files.

www.refugeecouncil.org.uk
The web pages of the largest refugee and asylum seeker organization in Great Britain.

http://www.un.org/en/rights/index.shtml
The United Nations page related to human rights includes links to UN reports and agencies, as well as an online version of the Universal Declaration of Human Rights.

http://www.freedomhouse.org
Freedom House is an independent watchdog organization dedicated to the expansion of freedom around the world. It rates the "progress and decline of political rights and civil liberties" in countries throughout the world.

www.unhcr.org
Official site of the United Nations High Commissioner for Refugees. The website has texts of all human rights treaties and details of UN proceedings (committee meetings, press briefings, etc).

Publisher's Note: The websites listed on these pages were active at the time of publication. The publisher is not responsible for websites that have changed their address or discontinued operation since the date of publication. The publisher reviews and updates the websites each time the book is reprinted.

Index

Numbers in ***bold italics*** refer to captions.

About the Author

Harry Miller studied English at Yale University and earned a graduate degree from the University of Phoenix. This is his first book.